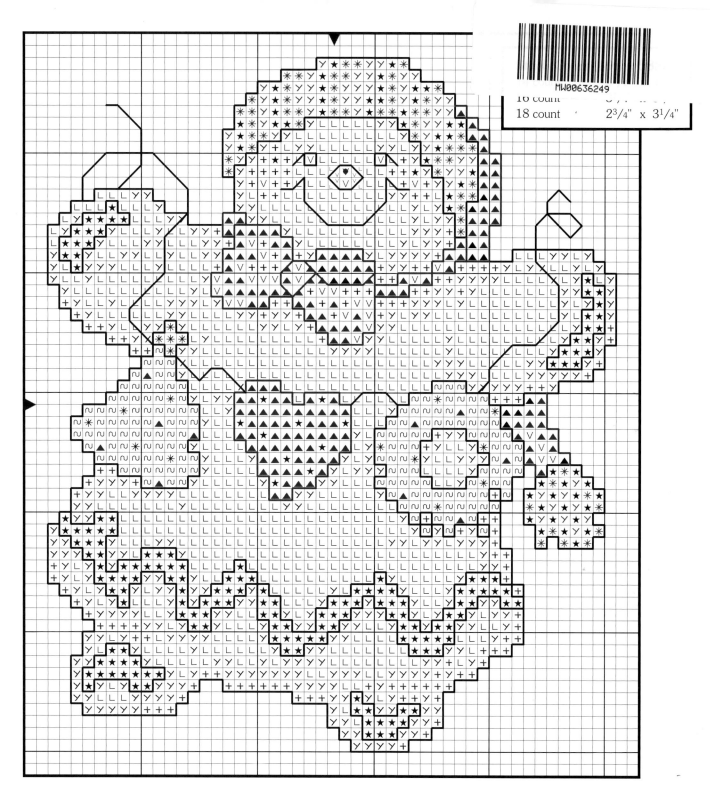

16 count
18 count   2³/₄" x 3¹/₄"

GINGERBREAD #1

X	DMC	ANC.	COLOR
★	blanc	2	white
▲	321	9046	red
V	351	10	peach
+	352	9	lt peach
+	434	310	golden brown
Y	436	1045	dk beige

X	DMC	¹/₄X	B'ST	ANC.	COLOR
L	437	◹		362	beige
✳	726			295	yellow
V	801	◿		359	brown
▲	816		╱	1005	maroon
✳	826			161	blue
Y	827			160	lt blue
∿	988			243	green
●	blanc			2	white Fr. Knot

Gingerbread #1 was stitched on a 6¹/₂" x 7¹/₂" piece of 14 count White Aida (design size 3¹/₂" x 4¹/₄"). Three strands of floss were used for Cross Stitch and one strand for Backstitch and French Knots.

Shown on page 26.

1

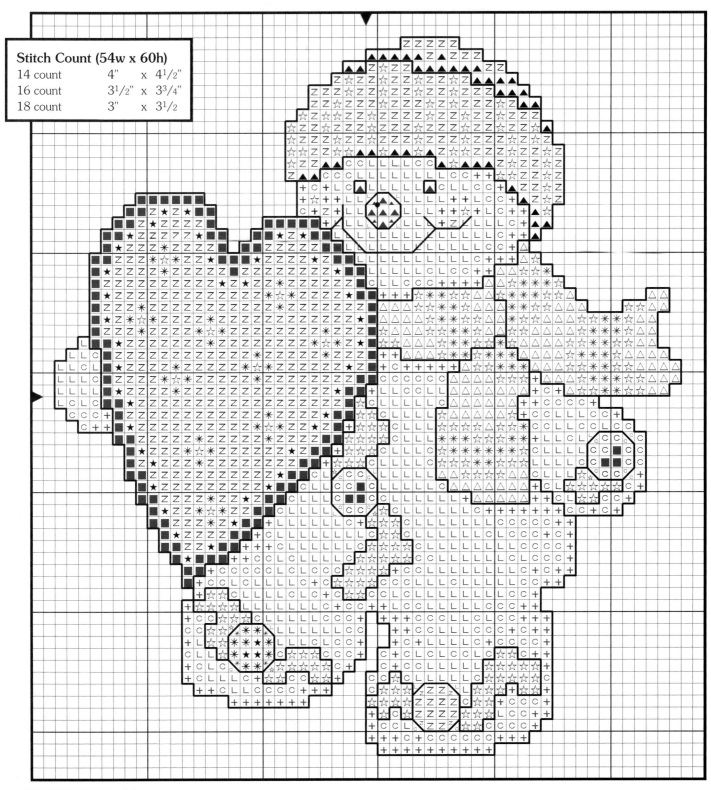

GINGERBREAD #2

X	DMC	1/4X	ANC.	COLOR
☆	blanc	☆	2	white
Z	321		9046	red
Z	351	z	10	peach
+	352		9	lt peach
+	434		310	golden brown
C	436	c	1045	dk beige
L	437	L	362	beige
✳	726	✳	295	yellow

X	DMC	1/4X	B'ST	ANC.	COLOR
★	783			306	gold
▲	801	▲	╱	359	brown
▲	816			1005	maroon
✳	826			161	blue
△	827			160	lt blue
■	987			244	lt green
C	989	c		242	dk green
●	blanc			2	white Fr. Knot

Gingerbread #2 was stitched on a 7" x 7½" piece of 14 count White Aida (design size 4" x 4½"). Three strands of floss were used for Cross Stitch and one strand for Backstitch and French Knots.

Shown on page 26.

Stitch Count (54w x 60h)

14 count	4"	x	4½"
16 count	3½"	x	3¾"
18 count	3"	x	3½"

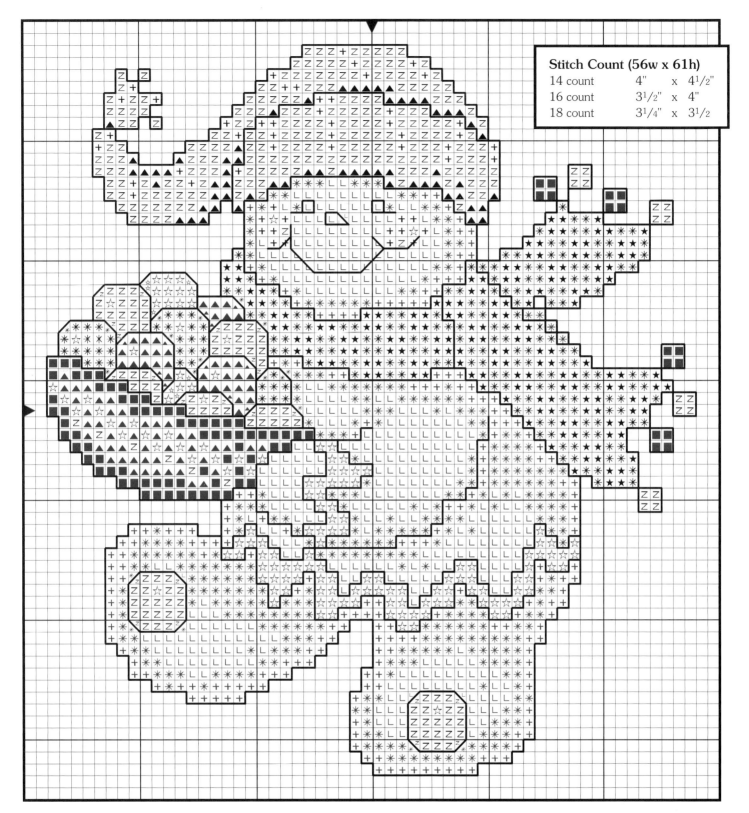

GINGERBREAD #3

X	DMC	1/4X	ANC.	COLOR
☆	blanc	◪	2	white
Z	321	◪	9046	red
Z	351		10	peach
+	352		9	lt peach
+	434		310	golden brown
✳	436	◪	1045	dk beige

X	DMC	1/4X	B'ST	ANC.	COLOR
L	437	◪		362	beige
✳	726	◪		295	yellow
★	783			306	gold
L	801	◪	╱	359	brown
▲	816			1005	maroon
■	987			244	green
▲	989	◪		242	dk green

Stitch Count (56w x 61h)

14 count	4"	x	4 1/2"
16 count	3 1/2"	x	4"
18 count	3 1/4"	x	3 1/2

Gingerbread #3 was stitched on a 7" x 7 1/2" piece of 14 count White Aida (design size 4" x 4 1/2"). Three strands of floss were used for Cross Stitch and one strand for Backstitch.

Shown on page 26.

3

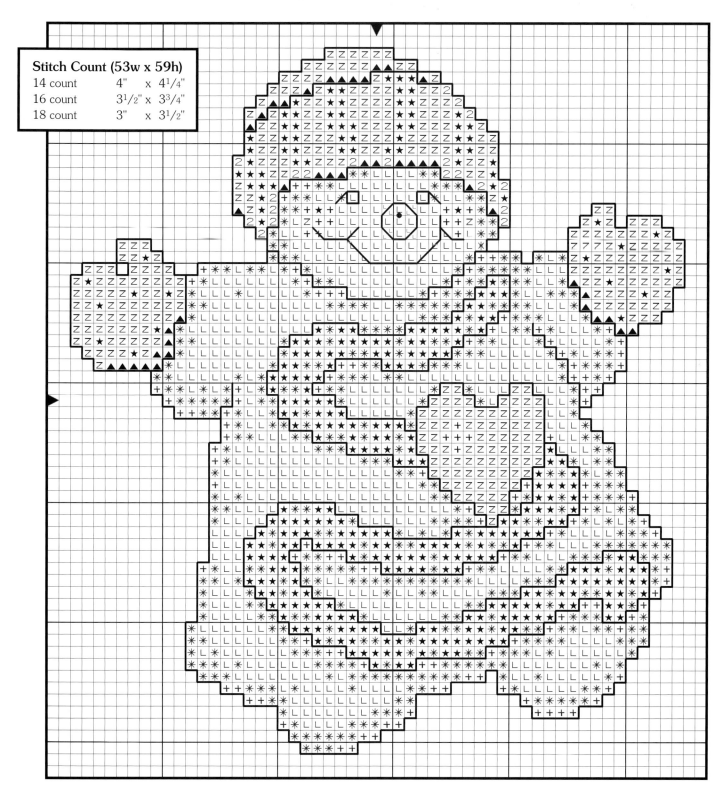

GINGERBREAD #4

X	DMC	ANC.	COLOR
★	blanc	2	white
Z	321	9046	red
Z	351	10	peach
+	352	9	lt peach
+	434	310	golden brown
✳	436	1045	dk beige

X	DMC	1/4X	B'ST	ANC.	COLOR
L	437	◣		362	beige
✳	702			226	lime green
Z	775			128	baby blue
L	801	◣	◢	359	brown
▲	816			1005	maroon
●	blanc			2	white Fr. Knot

Gingerbread #4 was stitched on a 7" x 7¼" piece of 14 count White Aida (design size 4" x 4¼"). Three strands of floss were used for Cross Stitch and one strand for Backstitch and French Knots.

Shown on page 26.

4

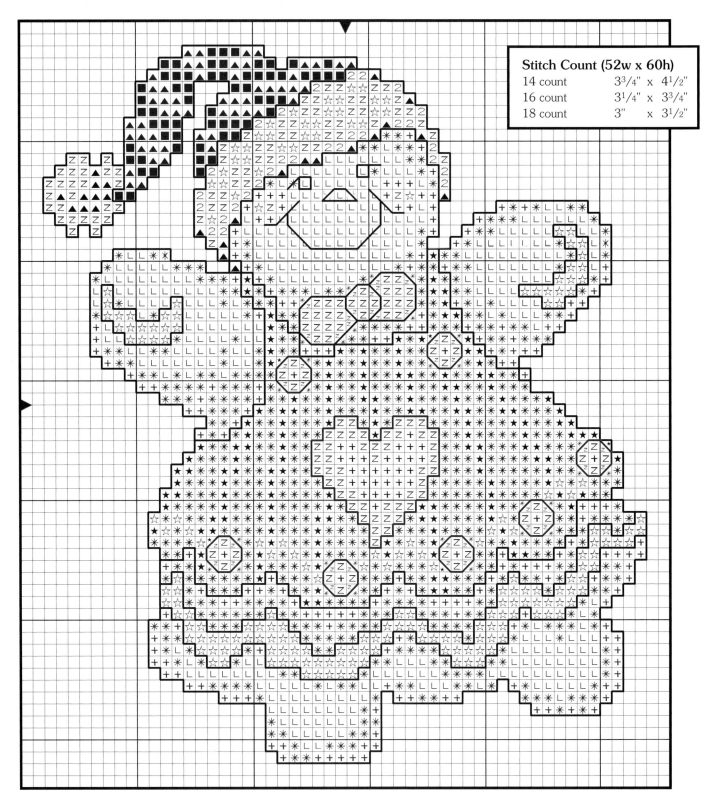

GINGERBREAD #5

X	DMC	1/4X	ANC.	COLOR
☆	blanc		2	white
Z	321	z	9046	red
Z	351		10	peach
+	352		9	lt peach
+	434		310	golden brown
*	436	*	1045	dk beige
L	437	L	362	beige

X	DMC	1/4X	B'ST	ANC.	COLOR
*	726	*		295	yellow
2	775			128	baby blue
★	783	*		306	gold
L	801	L	/	359	brown
▲	816		/	1005	maroon
■	987			244	green
▲	989			242	dk green

Gingerbread #5 was stitched on a 6³/₄" x 7¹/₂" piece of 14 count White Aida (design size 3³/₄" x 4¹/₂"). Three strands of floss were used for Cross Stitch and one strand for Backstitch.

Shown on page 26.

Stitch Count (52w x 60h)

14 count	3³/₄"	x	4¹/₂"
16 count	3¹/₄"	x	3³/₄"
18 count	3"	x	3¹/₂"

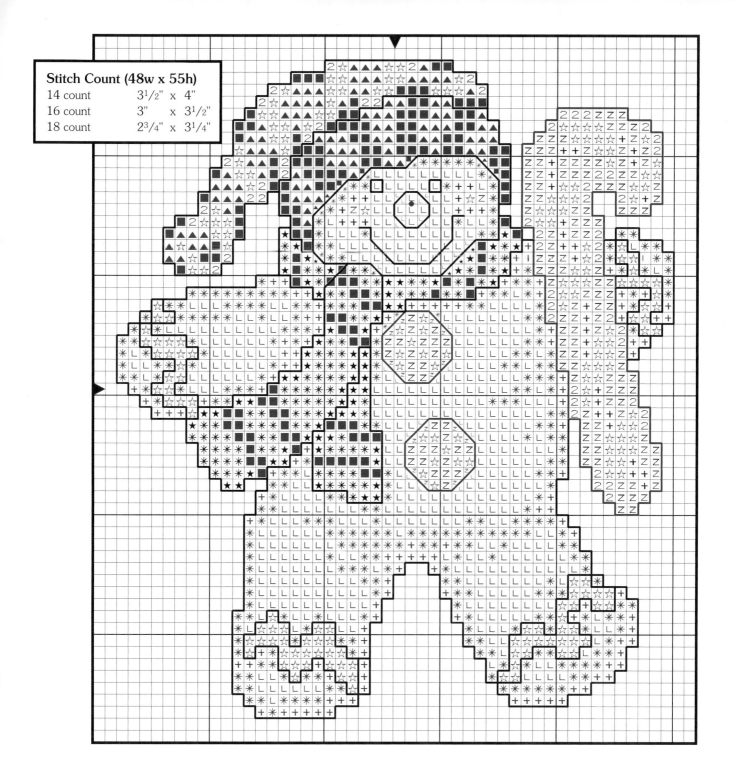

Stitch Count (48w x 55h)

14 count	3¹/₂"	x 4"
16 count	3"	x 3¹/₂"
18 count	2³/₄"	x 3¹/₄"

GINGERBREAD #6

X	DMC	¹/₄X	B'ST	ANC.	COLOR
☆	blanc			2	white
Z	321	z	/	9046	red
Z	351			10	peach
+	352			9	lt peach
+	434			310	golden brown
✳	436	✳		1045	dk beige
L	437	L		362	beige

X	DMC	¹/₄X	B'ST	ANC.	COLOR
✳	726	✳		295	yellow
2	775			128	baby blue
★	783	★		306	gold
L	801	L	/	359	brown
■	987	■		244	green
▲	989	▲		242	dk green
●	blanc			2	white Fr. Knot

Gingerbread #6 was stitched on a 6¹/₂" x 7" piece of 14 count White Aida (design size 3¹/₂" x 4"). Three strands of floss were used for Cross Stitch and one strand for Backstitch and French Knots.

Shown on page 26.

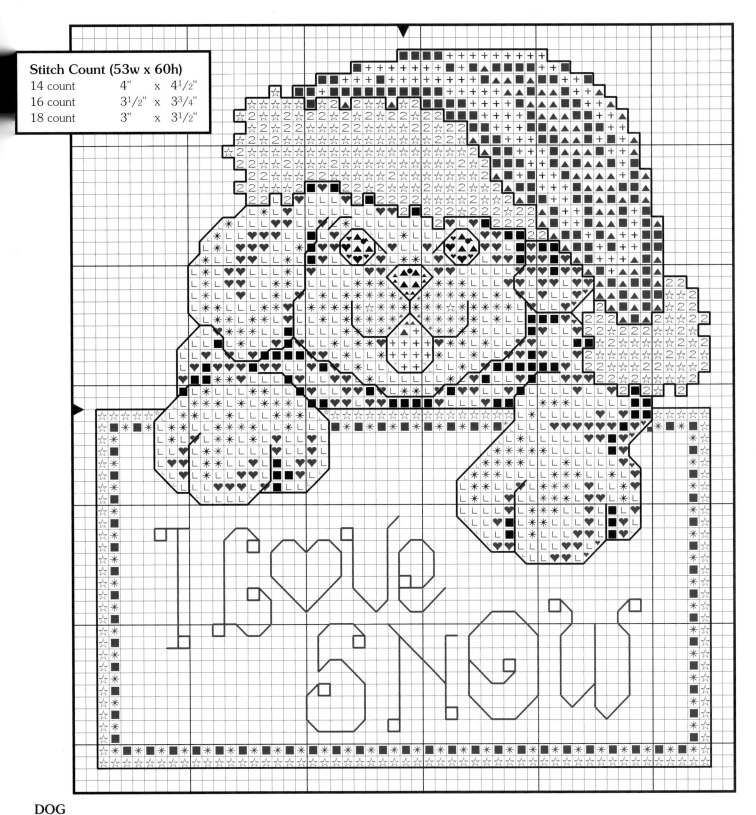

Stitch Count (53w x 60h)

14 count	4"	x	4 1/2"
16 count	3 1/2"	x	3 3/4"
18 count	3"	x	3 1/2"

DOG

X	DMC	1/4X	B'ST	ANC.	COLOR	X	DMC	1/4X	B'ST	ANC.	COLOR
☆	blanc			2	white	✳	712	✳		926	cream
▲	310	▲	/	403	black	✳	739	✳		387	dk cream
■	321	■		9046	red	▲	816	▲	/	1005	maroon
+	351	+		10	dk peach	■	898			360	brown
+	352			9	peach	♥	920	•		1004	orange
♥	435	•		1046	golden brown	2	3841			9159	baby blue
L	437	L		362	beige	●	blanc			2	white Fr. Knot
☆	702	☆		226	lt green						

Dog was stitched on a 7" x 7 1/2" piece of 14 count White Aida (design size 4" x 4 1/2"). Three strands of floss were used for Cross Stitch and one strand for Backstitch and French Knots.

Shown on page 24.

CAT

X	DMC	¹/₄X	B'ST	ANC.	COLOR	X	DMC	¹/₄X	B'ST	ANC.	COLOR
☆	blanc	◿		2	white	◐	415	◿		398	lt grey
▲	310	◣	╱	403	black	S	471	◿		266	lime green
✕	317			400	dk grey	☆	700	◿		228	green
L	318	◿		399	grey	2	762	◿		234	vy lt grey
■	321			9046	red	▲	816		╱	1005	maroon
+	351			10	dk peach	△	3841			9159	baby blue
+	352	◿		9	peach	●	blanc			2	white Fr. Knot
V	353			6	lt peach						

Cat was stitched on a 7" x 7¹/₂" piece of 14 count White Aida (design size 4" x 4¹/₂"). Three strands of floss were used for Cross Stitch and one strand for Backstitch and French Knots.

Shown on page 24.

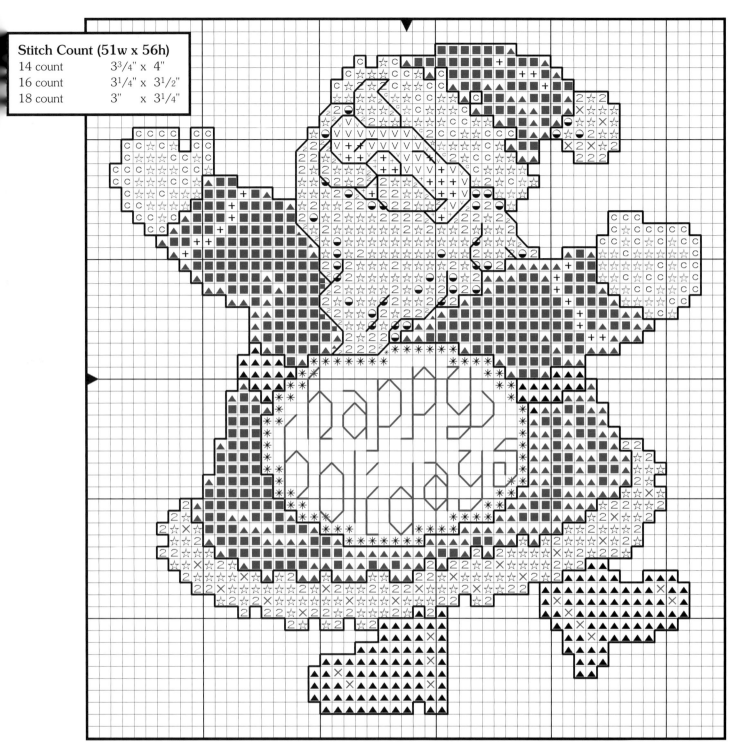

SANTA #1

X	DMC	1/4X	B'ST	ANC.	COLOR	X	DMC	1/4X	B'ST	ANC.	COLOR
☆	blanc	◪		2	white	◗	415			398	lt grey
▲	310		◿	403	black	✳	677	◿		886	lt gold
■	321	◪		9046	red	☆	701		◿	227	dk green
+	352	◿		9	peach	2	704	◿		256	lime green
V	353	◿		6	lt peach	2	762	◿		234	vy lt grey
✕	414			235	dk grey	▲	816	◿		1005	maroon

Santa #1 was stitched on a 6³/₄" x 7" piece of 14 count White Aida (design size 3³/₄" x 4"). Three strands of floss were used for Cross Stitch and one strand for Backstitch.

Shown on page 24.

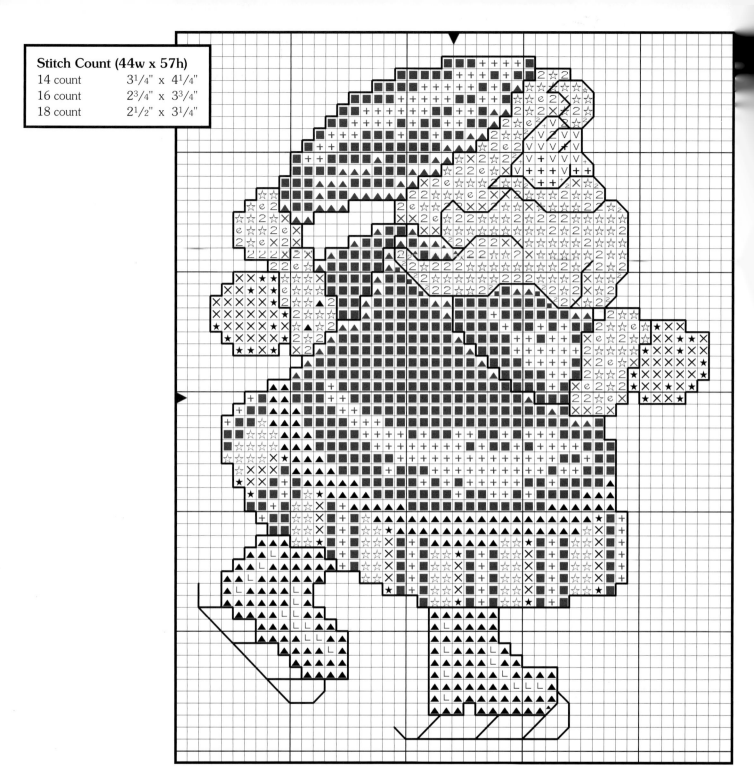

Stitch Count (44w x 57h)

14 count	3¼" x 4¼"
16 count	2¾" x 3¾"
18 count	2½" x 3¼"

SANTA #2

X	DMC	¼X	B'ST	ANC.	COLOR		X	DMC	¼X	ANC.	COLOR
☆	blanc	☆		2	white		L	414		235	dk grey
▲	310	▲	/	403	black		2	415	2	398	lt grey
☒	318	☒		399	grey		☆	702		226	green
■	321	■		9046	red		✕	726		295	yellow
+	351			10	dk peach		▲	816	▲	1005	maroon
+	352	◢		9	peach		e	930		1035	blue
V	353			6	lt peach		★	3852		306	dk gold

Santa #2 was stitched on a 6¼" x 7¼" piece of 14 count White Aida (design size 3¼" x 4¼"). Three strands of floss were used for Cross Stitch and one strand for Backstitch.

Shown on page 24.

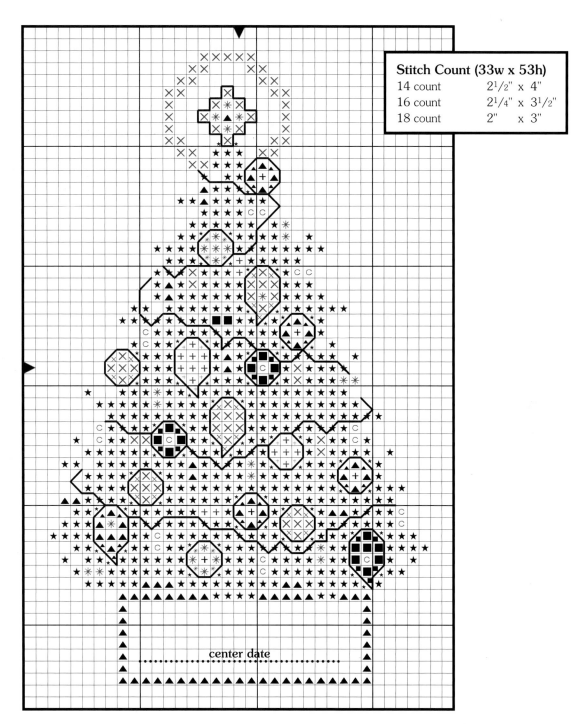

Stitch Count (33w x 53h)

14 count	2½" x 4"
16 count	2¼" x 3½"
18 count	2" x 3"

center date

TREE

X	DMC	¼X	B'ST	ANC.	COLOR
+	164	◪			sea green
	310		╱	403	black
▲	321	◪		9046	dk red
+	352			9	peach
★	702	◪		226	lime green
×	726	◪		295	yellow
■	798	◪		131	blue
C	809			130	lt blue
✳	947	◪		330	orange

Tree was stitched on a 5½" x 7" piece of 14 count White Aida (design size 2½" x 4"). Three strands of floss were used for Cross Stitch and one strand for Backstitch. Personalize using numeral chart #2 on page 46.

Shown on page 24.

BOY BOOTIES

X	DMC	¼X	B'ST	ANC.	COLOR
■	351			10	dk peach
	817		⧄	13	red
▲	911	◩		205	green
+	913			204	lt green
2	955			206	vy lt green
■	3818	◪	⧄	923	dk green

Boy Booties was stitched on a 6½" x 6½" piece of 14 count White Aida (design size 3½" x 3½"). Three strands of floss were used for Cross Stitch and one strand for Backstitch. Personalize using alphabet and numeral chart #1 on page 46.

Shown on page 24.

Stitch Count (48w x 47h)
14 count	3½" x 3½"
16 count	3" x 3"
18 count	2¾" x 2¾"

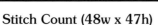

Stitch Count (34w x 38h)
14 count	2½" x 2¾"
16 count	2¼" x 2½"
18 count	2" x 2¼"

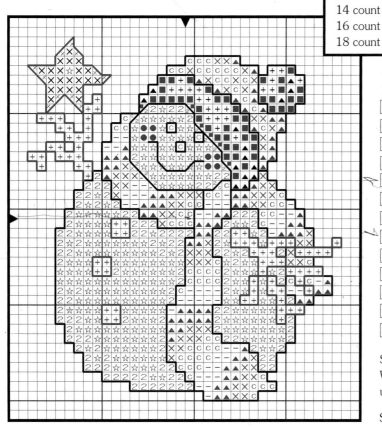

SNOWMAN #1

X	DMC	¼X	B'ST	ANC.	COLOR
☆	blanc			2	white
C	310		⧄	403	black
■	321	◪		9046	red
+	351			10	dk peach
●	353			6	peach
▲	700			228	green
✕	702	◩		226	dk lime green
C	704	◪		256	lime green
✕	726	◪		295	dk yellow
−	746	◪		275	lt yellow
▲	816			1005	maroon
+	920		⧄	1004	rust
2	3841	◪		9159	baby blue

Snowman #1 was stitched on a 6¼" x 6½" piece of 11 count White Aida (design size 3¼" x 3½"). Four strands of floss were used for Cross Stitch and one strand for Backstitch.

Shown on page 25.

GIRL BOOTIES

X	DMC	1/4X	B'ST	ANC.	COLOR
■	321	◿	◿	9046	dk red
C	351	◿c		10	dk peach
✚	352			9	peach
✚	353			6	lt peach
a	955			206	vy lt green
	3818		◿	923	dk green

Girl Booties was stitched on a 6¹/₂" x 6¹/₂" piece of 14 count White Aida (design size 3¹/₂" x 3¹/₂"). Three strands of floss were used for Cross Stitch and one strand for Backstitch. Personalize using alphabet and numeral chart #1 on page 46.

Shown on page 24.

Stitch Count (48w x 47h)		
14 count	3¹/₂"	x 3¹/₂"
16 count	3"	x 3"
18 count	2³/₄"	x 2³/₄"

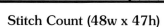

Stitch Count (39w x 39h)		
14 count	3"	x 3"
16 count	2¹/₂"	x 2¹/₂"
18 count	2¹/₄"	x 2¹/₄"

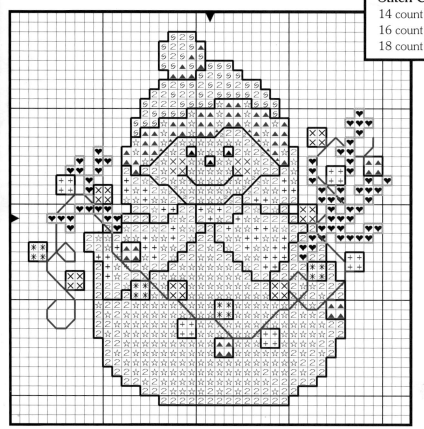

SNOWMAN #2

X	DMC	1/4X	B'ST	ANC.	COLOR
☆	blanc			2	white
▲	310		◿	403	black
2	321	◿2		9046	red
✚	351			10	dk peach
✕	353			6	peach
☆	677			886	gold
✳	701		◿	227	lt green
✕	726			295	dk yellow
▲	798	◿		131	blue
⑤	809			130	lt blue
♥	920		◿	1004	rust
✚	947			330	orange
2	3841	◿2		9159	baby blue

Snowman #2 was stitched on a 6" x 6" piece of 14 count White Aida (design size 3" x 3"). Three strands of floss were used for Cross Stitch and one strand for Backstitch.

Shown on page 25.

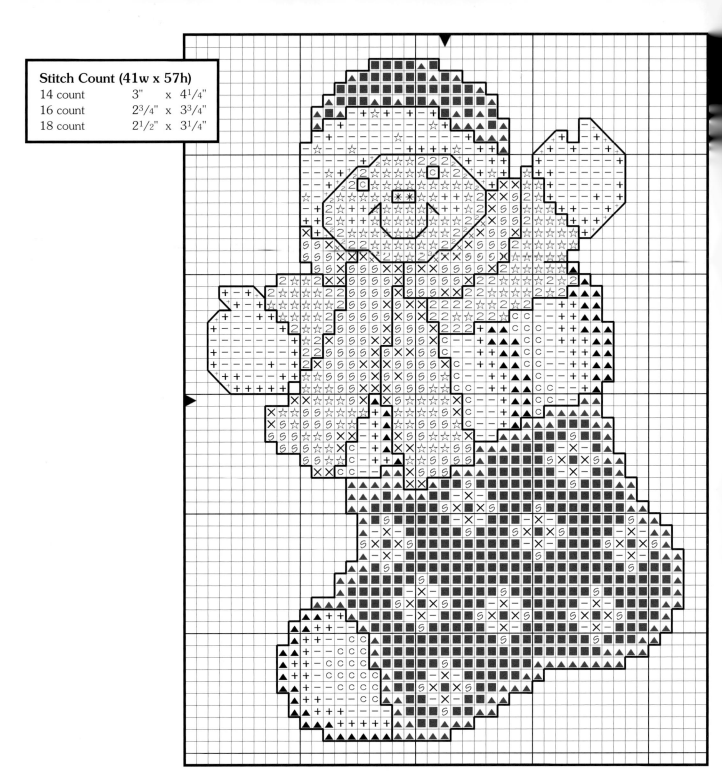

Stitch Count (41w x 57h)

14 count	3" x 4¼"
16 count	2¾" x 3¾"
18 count	2½" x 3¼"

SNOWMAN #3

X	DMC	¼X	B'ST	ANC.	COLOR
☆	blanc			2	white
C	164				sea green
C	310		╱	403	black
■	321			9046	red
+	353			6	peach
▲	700			228	green
+	702	╱		226	dk lime green

X	DMC	¼X	ANC.	COLOR
−	704		256	lime green
✕	726	╱	295	dk yellow
𝖲	727		293	yellow
2	775	╱	128	lt baby blue
▲	816		1005	maroon
✳	947		330	orange

Snowman #3 was stitched on a 6" x 7¼" piece of 14 count White Aida (design size 3" x 4¼"). Three strands of floss were used for Cross Stitch and one strand for Backstitch.

Shown on page 25.

14

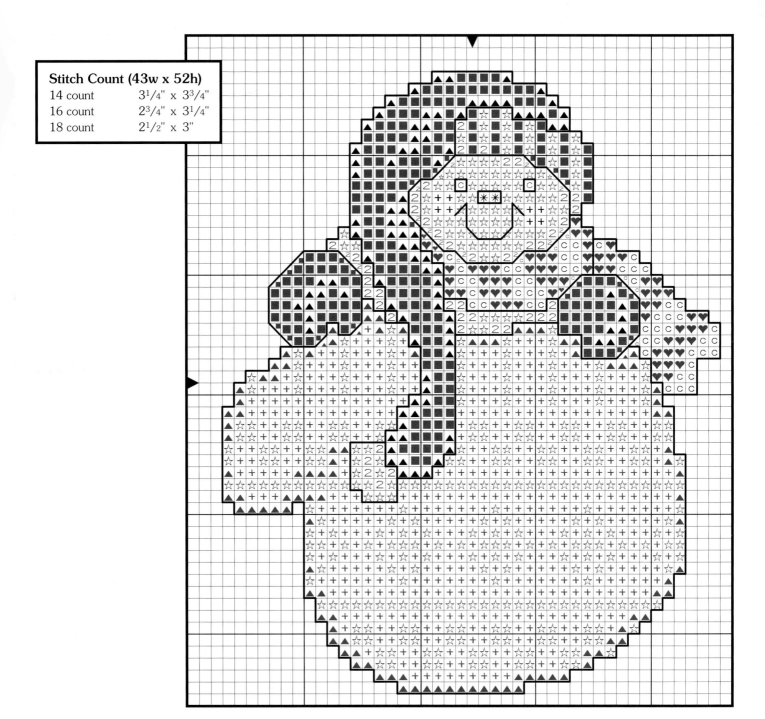

SNOWMAN #4

X	DMC	1/4X	B'ST	ANC.	COLOR		X	DMC	1/4X	ANC.	COLOR
☆	white	☆		2	white		2	775	2	128	baby blue
C	310		/	403	black		▲	796	◢	133	dk blue
■	321	◢		9046	red		+	798		131	blue
+	353			6	peach		▲	816		1005	maroon
♥	700	◢		228	green		✱	947		330	orange
C	704	◢		256	lt lime green						

Snowman #4 was stitched on a
6¼" x 6¾" piece of 14 count
White Aida (design size 3¼" x 3¾").
Three strands of floss were used for
Cross Stitch and one strand for Backstitch.

Shown on page 25.

Stitch Count (43w x 52h)
14 count	3¼" x 3¾"
16 count	2¾" x 3¼"
18 count	2½" x 3"

15

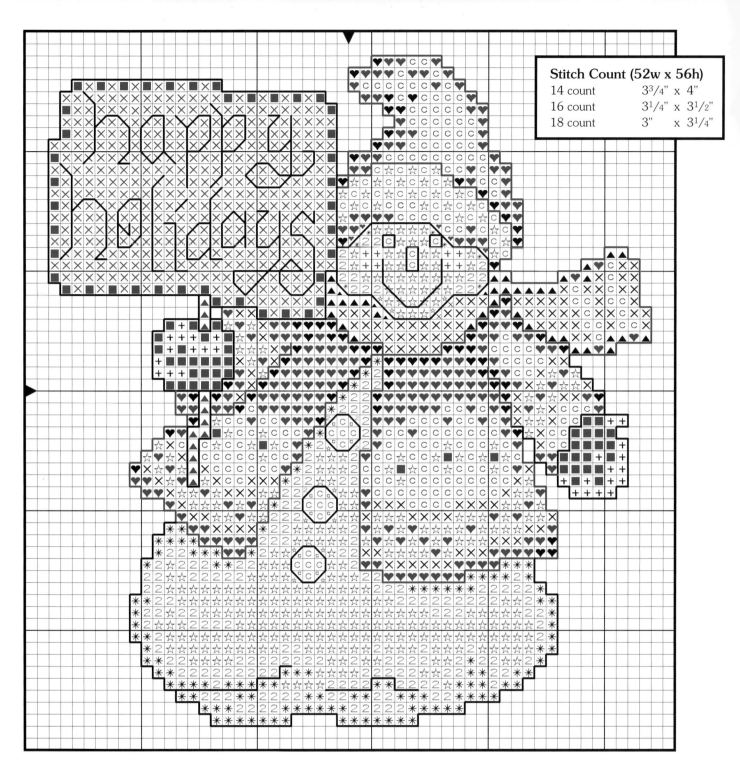

Stitch Count (52w x 56h)

14 count	3³/₄"	x 4"
16 count	3¹/₄"	x 3¹/₂"
18 count	3"	x 3¹/₄"

SNOWMAN #5

X	DMC	¹/₄X	B'ST	ANC.	COLOR
☆	white			2	white
C	310		/	403	black
■	321			9046	red
+	351			10	dk peach
+	353			6	peach
▲	433			358	brown
♥	700		/	228	green

X	DMC	¹/₄X	ANC.	COLOR
♥	702		226	lime green
C	704		256	lt lime green
X	726		295	yellow
X	746		275	cream
2	775		128	baby blue
✳	932		1033	blue grey
▲	3820		306	gold

Snowman #5 was stitched on a 6³/₄" x 7" piece of 14 count Red Aida (design size 3³/₄" x 4"). Three strands of floss were used for Cross Stitch and one strand for Backstitch.

Shown on page 25.

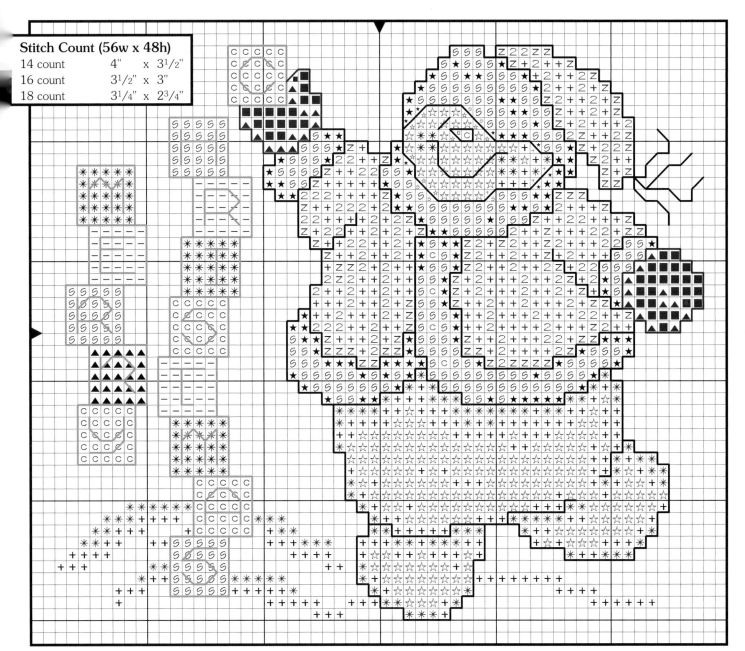

SNOWMAN #6

X	DMC	1/4X	B'ST	ANC.	COLOR
☆	white	☆		2	white
C	164				sea green
C	310	c	/	403	black
■	321	■		9046	red
✳	353			6	peach
▲	677			886	lt gold
S	726	S		295	yellow
–	746			275	cream

X	DMC	1/4X	B'ST	ANC.	COLOR
+	775	+		128	baby blue
Z	796			133	dk blue
+	798			131	blue
2	809			130	lt blue
▲	816		/	1005	maroon
	895		/	1044	green
✳	932			1033	blue grey
★	3852	★		306	dk gold

Snowman #6 was stitched on a 7" x 6½" piece of 14 count White Aida (design size 4" x 3½"). Three strands of floss were used for Cross Stitch and one strand for Backstitch.

Shown on page 25.

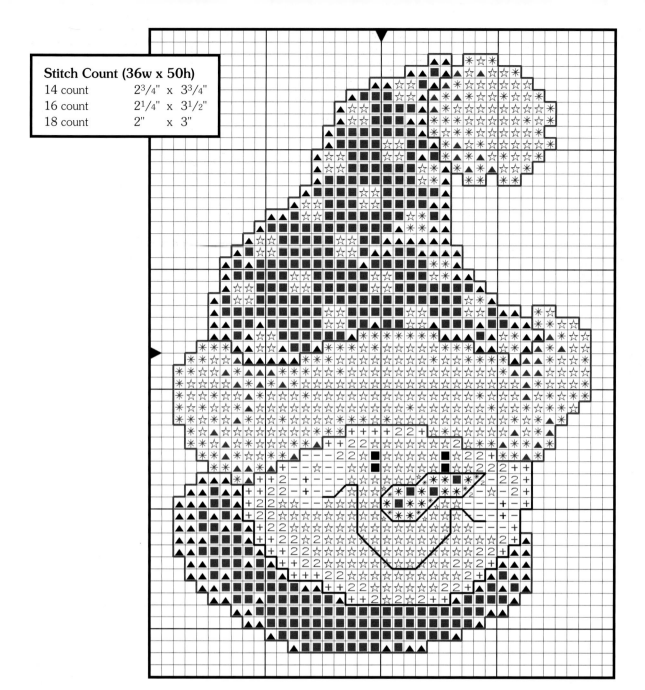

Stitch Count (36w x 50h)

14 count	$2^3/_4$" x $3^3/_4$"
16 count	$2^1/_4$" x $3^1/_2$"
18 count	2" x 3"

SNOWMAN #7

X	DMC	¼X	B'ST	ANC.	COLOR		X	DMC	¼X	B'ST	ANC.	COLOR
☆	blanc	☆		2	white		✳	739			387	beige
■	310		/	403	black		2	775	2		128	baby blue
■	321			9046	red		▲	816		/	1005	maroon
+	352			9	peach		+	932			1033	grey blue
−	353			6	lt peach		✳	947	✳		330	orange
▲	436			1045	golden brown							

Snowman #7 was stitched on a 5$^3/_4$" x 6$^3/_4$" piece of 14 count White Aida (design size 2$^3/_4$" x 3$^3/_4$"). Three strands of floss were used for Cross Stitch and one strand for Backstitch.

Shown on page 25.

18

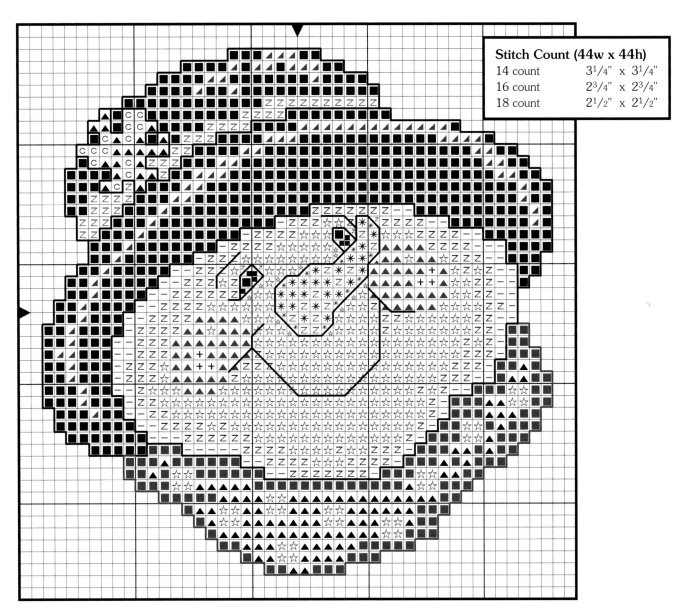

Stitch Count (44w x 44h)

14 count	$3^1/4$"	x $3^1/4$"
16 count	$2^3/4$"	x $2^3/4$"
18 count	$2^1/2$"	x $2^1/2$"

SNOWMAN #8

X	DMC	¼X	B'ST	ANC.	COLOR	X	DMC	¼X	B'ST	ANC.	COLOR
☆	blanc	☆		2	white	■	700		╱	228	green
■	310	▪	╱	403	black	▲	702			226	lime green
◢	318			399	grey	C	704			256	lt lime green
Z	321			9046	red	Z	775	z		128	baby blue
+	352			9	peach	−	932			1033	grey blue
▲	353	◢		6	lt peach	✱	947	✻		330	orange

Snowman #8 was stitched on a
$6^1/4$" x $6^1/4$" piece of 14 count Red Aida
(design size $3^1/4$" x $3^1/4$"). Three strands
of floss were used for Cross Stitch
and one strand for Backstitch.

Shown on page 25.

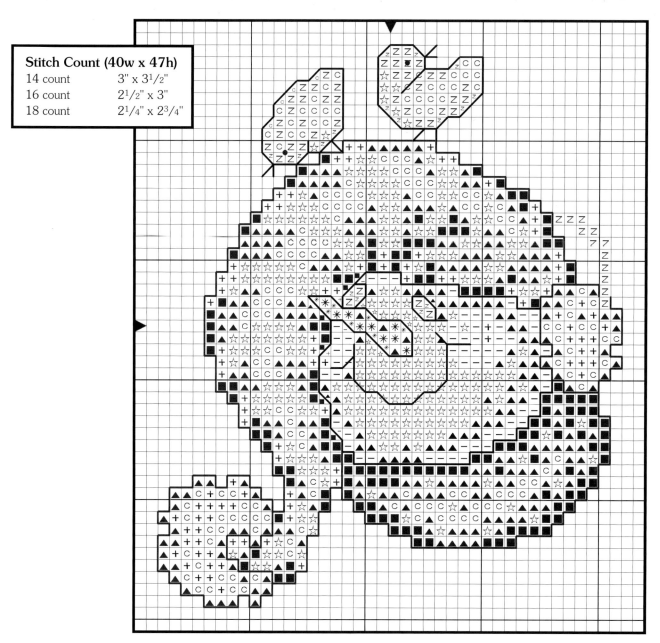

SNOWMAN #9

X	DMC	¹/₄X	B'ST	ANC.	COLOR	X	DMC	¹/₄X	B'ST	ANC.	COLOR
☆	blanc	☆		2	white	+	739	+		387	beige
Z	310	z	/	403	black	Z	762	z		234	lt grey
C	318	c		399	grey	▲	775	▲		128	baby blue
▲	321	▲		9046	red	■	816	■	/	1005	maroon
C	351			10	dk peach	–	932	–		1033	grey blue
+	352	+		9	peach	✳	947	✳		330	orange
–	353			6	lt peach	●	310			403	black Fr. Knot

Snowman #9 was stitched on a 6" x 6¹/₂" piece of 14 count White Aida (design size 3" x 3¹/₂"). Three strands of floss were used for Cross Stitch and one strand for Backstitch and French Knots.

Shown on page 25.

Stitch Count (40w x 47h)

14 count	3" x 3¹/₂"
16 count	2¹/₂" x 3"
18 count	2¹/₄" x 2³/₄"

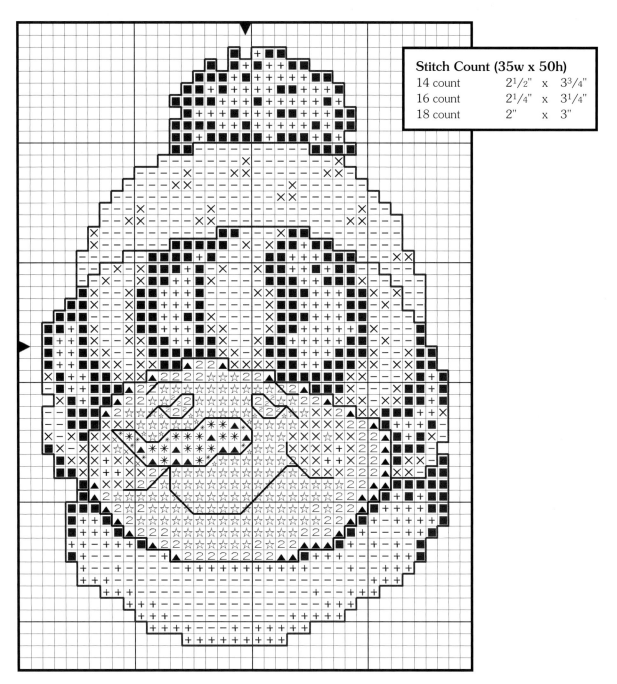

Stitch Count (35w x 50h)

14 count	2¹/₂"	x 3³/₄"
16 count	2¹/₄"	x 3¹/₄"
18 count	2"	x 3"

SNOWMAN #10

X	DMC	¹/₄X	B'ST	ANC.	COLOR		X	DMC	¹/₄X	B'ST	ANC.	COLOR
☆	blanc	☆		2	white		–	704			256	lt lime green
2	310	2	/	403	black		✕	726			295	dk yellow
▲	321			9046	red		–	727			293	yellow
+	352			9	peach		2	775	2		128	baby blue
✕	353	✕		6	lt peach			895		/	1044	dk green
■	700			228	green		▲	932			1033	grey blue
+	702			226	lime green		✳	947	✳		330	orange

Snowman #10 was stitched on a 5¹/₂" x 6³/₄" piece of 14 count Red Aida (design size 2¹/₂" x 3³/₄"). Three strands of floss were used for Cross Stitch and one strand for Backstitch.

Shown on page 25.

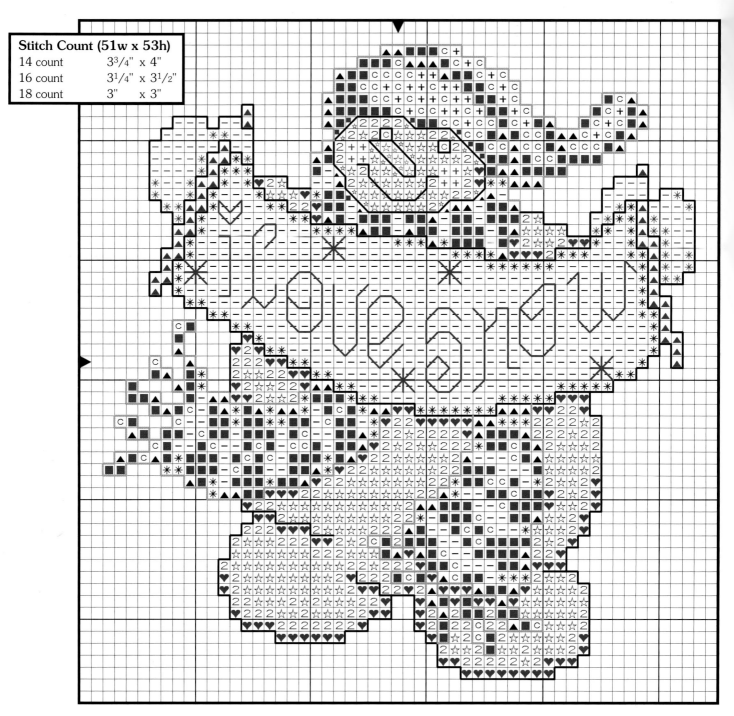

SNOWMAN #11

Snowman #11 was stitched on a 6³/₄" x 6³/₄" piece of 14 count White Aida (design size 3³/₄" x 4"). Three strands of floss were used for Cross Stitch and one strand for Backstitch.

Shown on page 25.

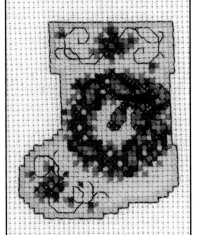
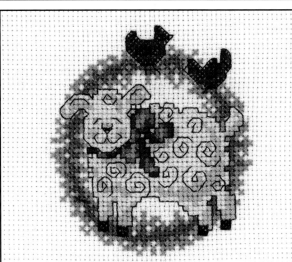

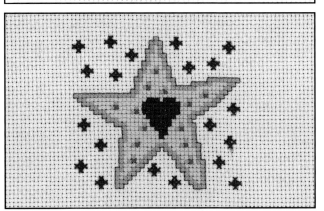
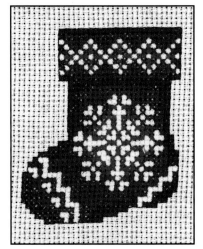
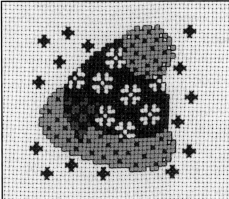
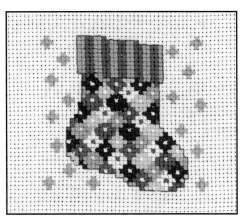

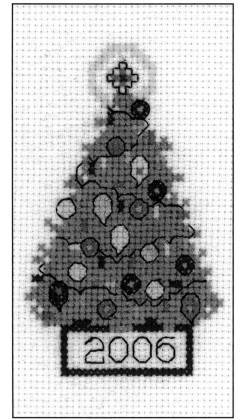

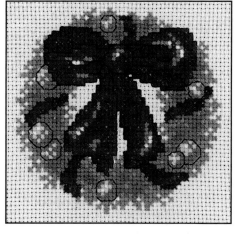

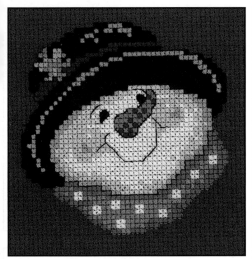

Stitch Count (41w x 37h)

14 count	3"	x	2³/₄"
16 count	2³/₄"	x	2¹/₂"
18 count	2¹/₂"	x	2¹/₄"

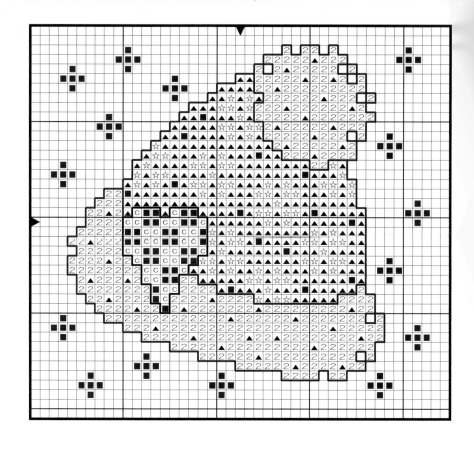

Hat was stitched on a 6" x 5³/₄" piece of 14 count White Aida (design size 3" x 2³/₄"). Three strands of floss were used for Cross Stitch and one strand for Backstitch.

HAT

X	DMC	B'ST	ANC.	COLOR
☆	blanc		2	white
■	321	/	9046	red
C	351		10	peach
▲	796	/	133	blue
2	809		130	lt blue

Shown on page 23.

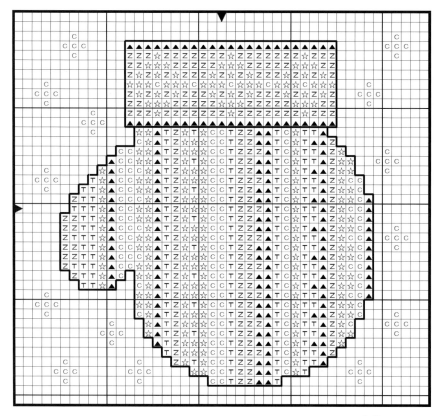

Stitch Count (41w x 37h)

14 count	3"	x	2³/₄"
16 count	2³/₄"	x	2¹/₂"
18 count	2¹/₂"	x	2¹/₄"

Mitten was stitched on a 6" x 5³/₄" piece of 14 count White Aida (design size 3" x 2³/₄"). Three strands of floss were used for Cross Stitch and one strand for Backstitch.

MITTEN

X	DMC	B'ST	ANC.	COLOR
☆	blanc		2	white
Z	321		9046	red
C	704		256	lime green
▲	796	/	133	blue
T	809		130	lt blue

Shown on page 23.

Stitch Count (41w x 37h)

14 count	3"	x	2³/₄"
16 count	2³/₄"	x	2¹/₂"
18 count	2¹/₂"	x	2¹/₄"

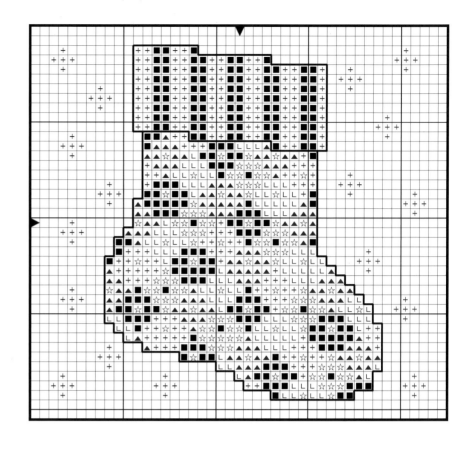

Stocking #1 was stitched on a 6" x 5³/₄" piece of 14 count White Aida (design size 3" x 2³/₄"). Three strands of floss were used for Cross Stitch and one strand for Backstitch.

STOCKING #1

X	DMC	B'ST	ANC.	COLOR
☆	blanc		2	white
▲	321		9046	red
■	700	╱	228	green
+	704		256	lime green
L	726		295	yellow

Shown on page 23.

Stitch Count (41w x 37h)

14 count	3"	x	2³/₄"
16 count	2³/₄"	x	2¹/₂"
18 count	2¹/₂"	x	2¹/₄"

Star was stitched on a 6" x 5³/₄" piece of 14 count White Aida (design size 3" x 2³/₄"). Three strands of floss were used for Cross Stitch and one strand for Backstitch.

STAR

X	DMC	B'ST	ANC.	COLOR
▲	321	╱	2	red
■	700	╱	228	green
+	704		256	lime green
L	726		295	yellow

Shown on page 23.

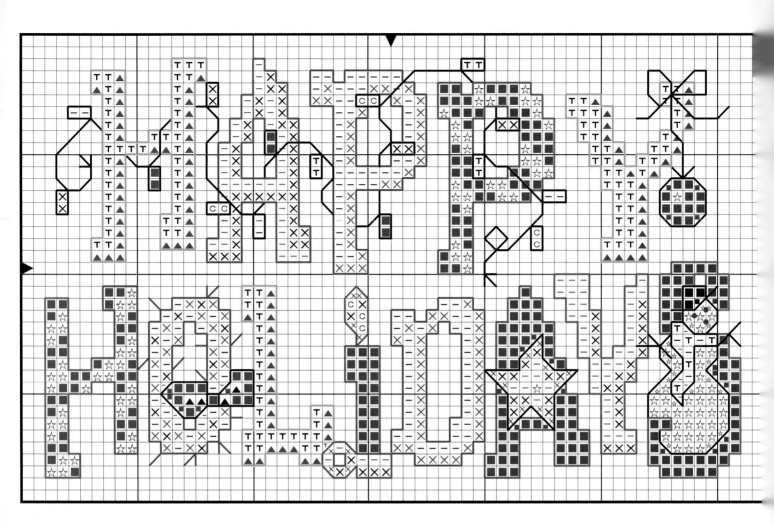

HAPPY HOLIDAYS

X	DMC	1/4X	B'ST	ANC.	COLOR
☆	blanc			2	white
■	310			403	black
■	321			9046	red
✕	700			228	green
−	702			226	lime green
✕	726			295	dk yellow
−	727			293	yellow
▲	796			133	dk blue
T	798			131	blue
▲	816			1005	maroon
C	947			330	orange
●	310			403	black Fr. Knot

Happy Holidays was stitched on a 7¹/₂" x 5¹/₂" piece of 14 count White Aida (design size 4¹/₂" x 2¹/₂"). Three strands of floss were used for Cross Stitch and one strand for Backstitch and French Knots.

Stitch Count (60w x 35h)		
14 count	4¹/₂"	x 2¹/₂"
16 count	3³/₄"	x 2¹/₄"
18 count	3¹/₂"	x 2"

Shown on page 26.

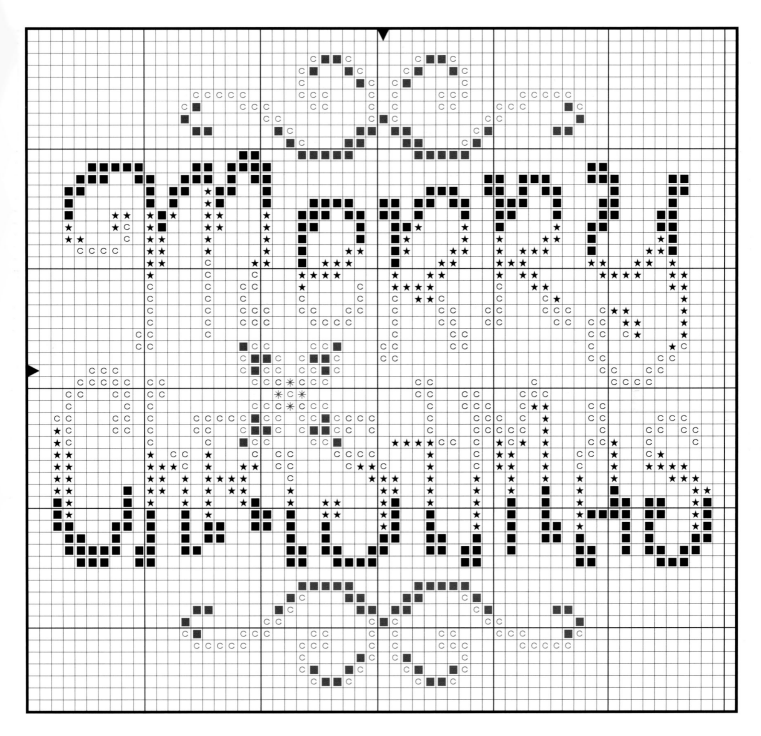

MERRY CHRISTMAS

X	DMC	ANC.	COLOR
C	321	9046	red
■	700	228	green
★	702	226	lime green
C	704	256	lt lime green
✳	726	295	yellow
■	816	1005	maroon

Merry Christmas was stitched on a 7¹/₄" x 7" piece of 14 count White Aida (design size 4¹/₄" x 4"). Three strands of floss were used for Cross Stitch.

Stitch Count (57w x 53h)		
14 count	4¹/₄" x	4"
16 count	3³/₄" x	3¹/₂"
18 count	3¹/₄" x	3"

Shown on page 26.

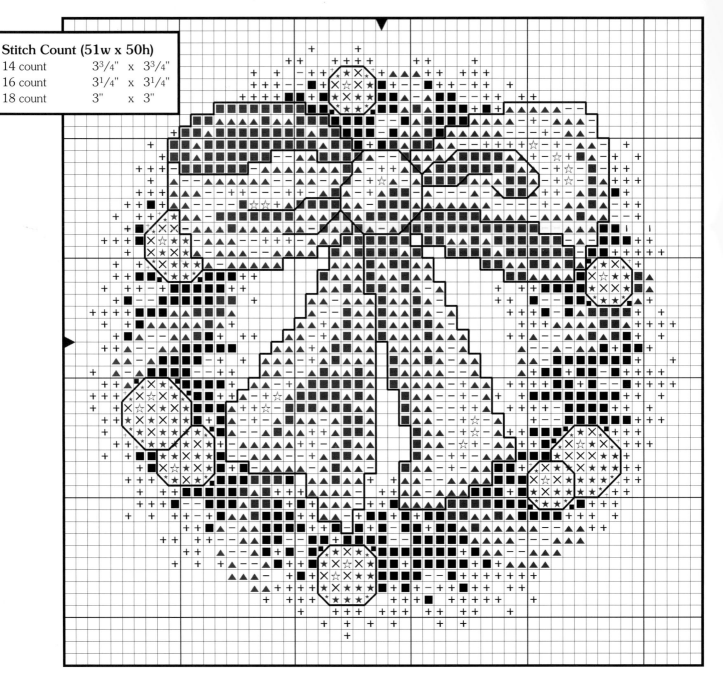

Stitch Count (51w x 50h)

14 count	$3^{3}/_{4}$"	x $3^{3}/_{4}$"
16 count	$3^{1}/_{4}$"	x $3^{1}/_{4}$"
18 count	3"	x 3"

WREATH

X	DMC	¹/₄X	B'ST	ANC.	COLOR
☆	blanc			2	white
	310		╱	403	black
▲	321			9046	red
−	350			11	peach
+	352			9	lt peach
✕	726			295	yellow
★	782	╱		307	gold
−	798			131	blue
■	816			1005	maroon
■	3346	╱		267	dk avocado green
+	3347	╱		266	avocado green

Wreath was stitched on a $6^{3}/_{4}$" x $6^{3}/_{4}$" piece of 14 count White Aida (design size $3^{3}/_{4}$" x $3^{3}/_{4}$"). Three strands of floss were used for Cross Stitch and one strand for Backstitch.

Shown on page 24.

HOUSE

X DMC	1/4X	B'ST	ANC.	COLOR
☆ blanc	◹		2	white
■ 321	◪		9046	red
+ 352			9	lt peach
■ 435	◪		1046	golden brown
− 677			886	lt gold
699		╱	923	dk green
C 703	◿c		238	lt lime green
✕ 726	◹✕		295	yellow
816		╱	1005	maroon

House was stitched on a 5 1/2" x 6" piece of 14 count White Aida (design size 2 1/2" x 3"). Three strands of floss were used for Cross Stitch and one strand for Backstitch.

Shown on page 24.

Stitch Count (35w x 39h)

14 count	2 1/2" x	3"
16 count	2 1/4" x	2 1/2"
18 count	2" x	2 1/4"

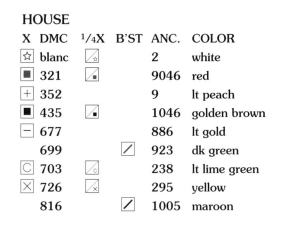

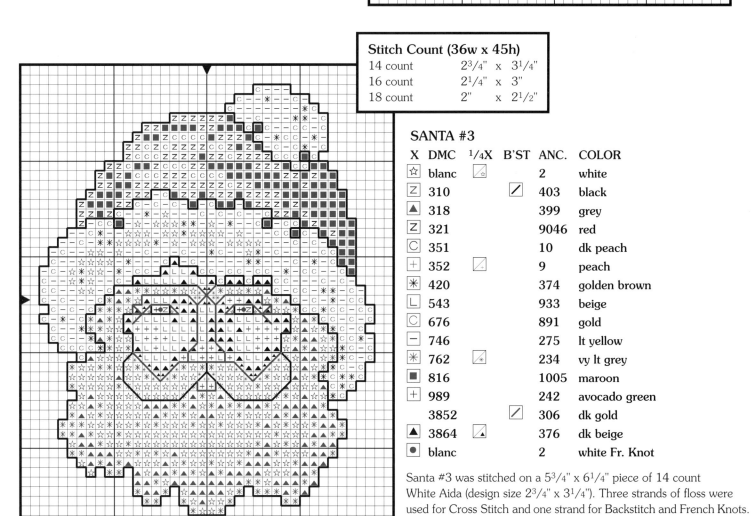

Stitch Count (36w x 45h)

14 count	2 3/4" x	3 1/4"
16 count	2 1/4" x	3"
18 count	2" x	2 1/2"

SANTA #3

X DMC	1/4X	B'ST	ANC.	COLOR
☆ blanc	◹		2	white
Z 310		╱	403	black
▲ 318			399	grey
Z 321			9046	red
C 351			10	dk peach
+ 352		◿	9	peach
✳ 420			374	golden brown
L 543			933	beige
C 676			891	gold
− 746			275	lt yellow
✳ 762	◿✳		234	vy lt grey
■ 816			1005	maroon
+ 989			242	avocado green
3852		╱	306	dk gold
▲ 3864	◹▲		376	dk beige
● blanc			2	white Fr. Knot

Santa #3 was stitched on a 5 3/4" x 6 1/4" piece of 14 count White Aida (design size 2 3/4" x 3 1/4"). Three strands of floss were used for Cross Stitch and one strand for Backstitch and French Knots.

Shown on page 27.

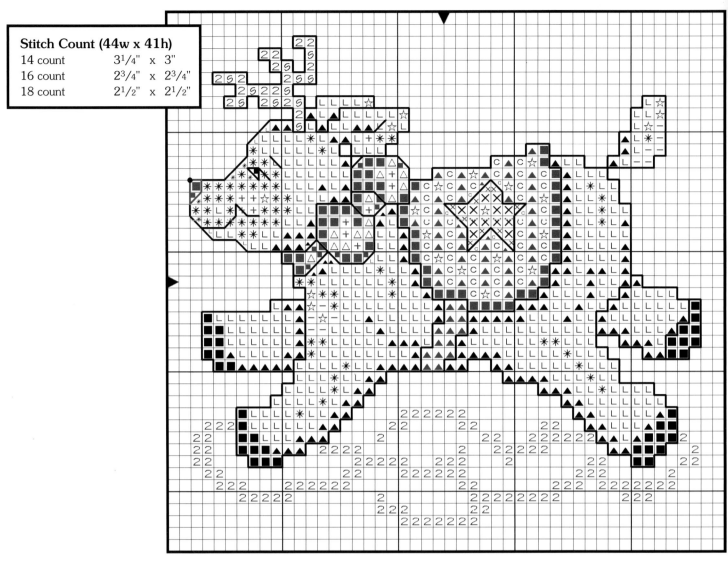

REINDEER #1

X	DMC	¼X	B'ST	ANC.	COLOR
☆	blanc			2	white
■	321	◩	╱	9046	red
△	351			10	dk peach
+	352			9	peach
▲	435	◪		1046	golden brown
L	437	◪		362	beige
▲	702	◪		226	green
C	704	◪		256	lime green

X	DMC	¼X	B'ST	ANC.	COLOR
✕	726	◪		295	yellow
✳	739	◪		387	beige
−	746			275	lt yellow
2	775			128	baby blue
5	809			130	blue
■	3371	◩	╱	382	dk brown
●	blanc			2	white Fr. Knot

Reindeer #1 was stitched on a 6¼" x 6" piece of 14 count White Aida (design size 3¼" x 3"). Three strands of floss were used for Cross Stitch and one strand for Backstitch and French Knots.

Shown on page 27.

Stitch Count (44w x 41h)

14 count	3¼"	x	3"
16 count	2¾"	x	2¾"
18 count	2½"	x	2½"

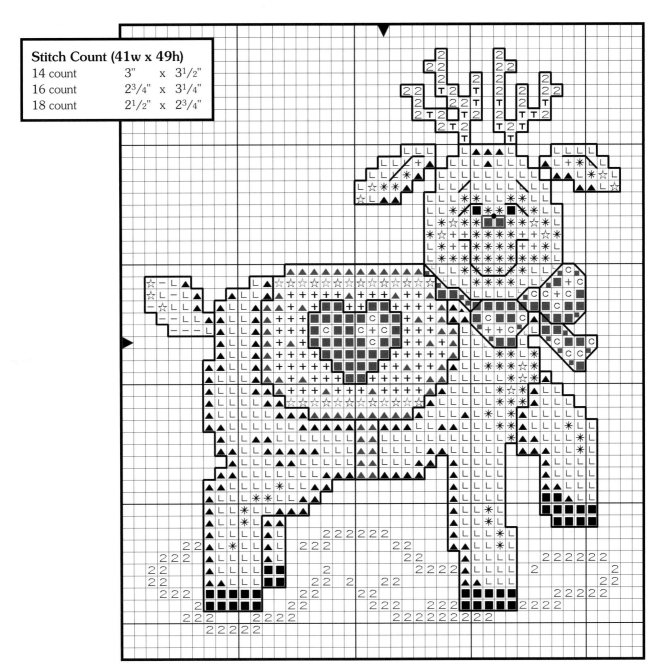

REINDEER #2

X	DMC	1/4X	B'ST	ANC.	COLOR
☆	blanc			2	white
■	321	◢	╱	9046	red
©	351			10	dk peach
+	352			9	peach
▲	435	◢		1046	golden brown
L	437	◣		362	beige
▲	702			226	green
✳	739			387	beige

X	DMC	B'ST	ANC.	COLOR
−	746		275	lt yellow
+	772		259	lt green
2	775		128	baby blue
T	809		130	blue
■	3371	╱	382	dk brown
☆	3820		306	gold
●	blanc		2	white Fr. Knot

Stitch Count (41w x 49h)

14 count	3"	x	3½"
16 count	2¾"	x	3¼"
18 count	2½"	x	2¾"

Reindeer #2 was stitched on a 6" x 6½" piece of 14 count White Aida (design size 3" x 3½"). Three strands of floss were used for Cross Stitch and one strand for Backstitch and French Knots.

Shown on page 27.

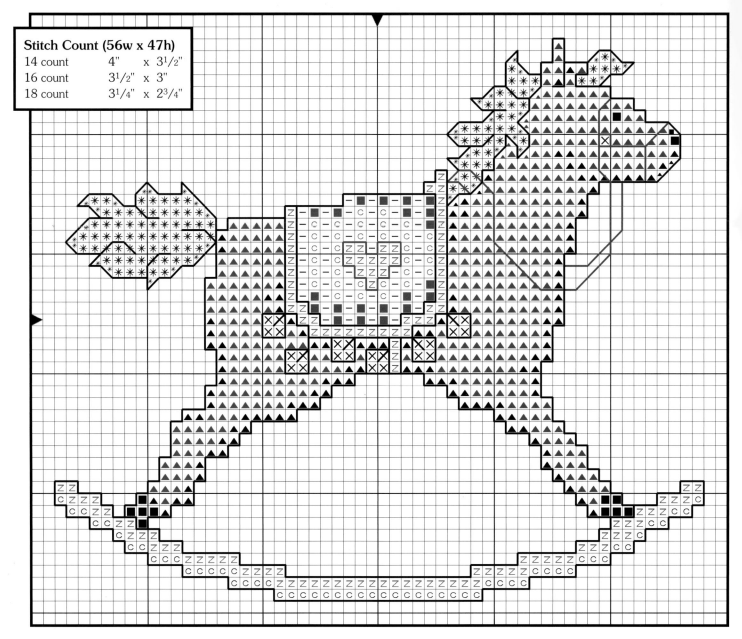

Stitch Count (56w x 47h)
14 count	4"	x 3½"
16 count	3½"	x 3"
18 count	3¼"	x 2¾"

ROCKING HORSE

X	DMC	¼X	B'ST	ANC.	COLOR
Z	321			9046	red
■	700			228	green
C	702			226	dk lime green
X	726			295	dk yellow
✳	739	╱		387	beige
−	746			275	lt yellow
C	816		╱	1005	maroon
▲	920	╱		1004	rust
▲	922	╱		1003	lt rust
■	3371	╱	╱	382	dk brown

Rocking Horse was stitched on a 7" x 6½" piece of 14 count White Aida (design size 4" x 3½"). Three strands of floss were used for Cross Stitch and one strand for Backstitch.

Shown on page 23.

36

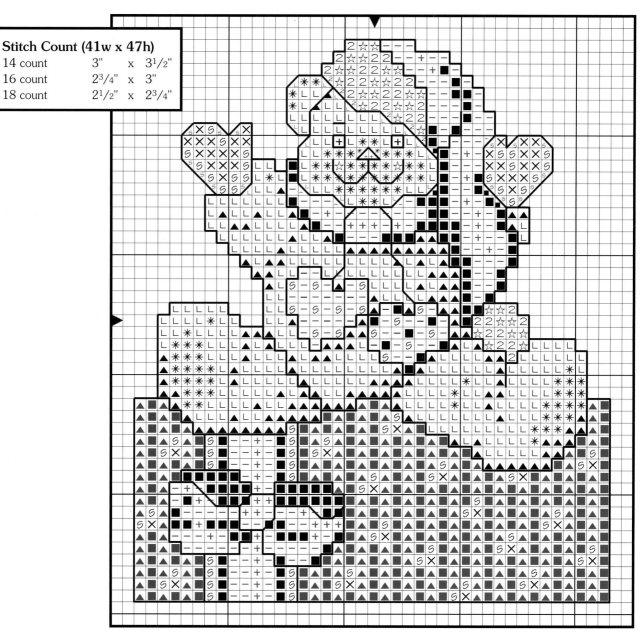

<table>
<tr><td colspan="4">Stitch Count (41w x 47h)</td></tr>
<tr><td>14 count</td><td>3"</td><td>x</td><td>3¹/₂"</td></tr>
<tr><td>16 count</td><td>2³/₄"</td><td>x</td><td>3"</td></tr>
<tr><td>18 count</td><td>2¹/₂"</td><td>x</td><td>2³/₄"</td></tr>
</table>

BEAR

X	DMC	¹/₄X	B'ST	ANC.	COLOR
☆	blanc			2	white
+	310	◿	◿	403	black
–	321	◿		9046	red
+	351			10	dk peach
▲	435			1046	golden brown
L	437	◿		362	lt golden brown
–	676			891	gold
■	702			226	dk lime green
▲	704			256	lt lime green
✕	726			295	dk yellow
S	727	◿		293	yellow
✳	739	◿		387	beige
2	775	◿		128	baby blue
■	816	◿		1005	maroon

Bear was stitched on a 6" x 6¹/₂" piece of 14 count White Aida (design size 3" x 3¹/₂"). Three strands of floss were used for Cross Stitch and one strand for Backstitch.

Shown on page 24.

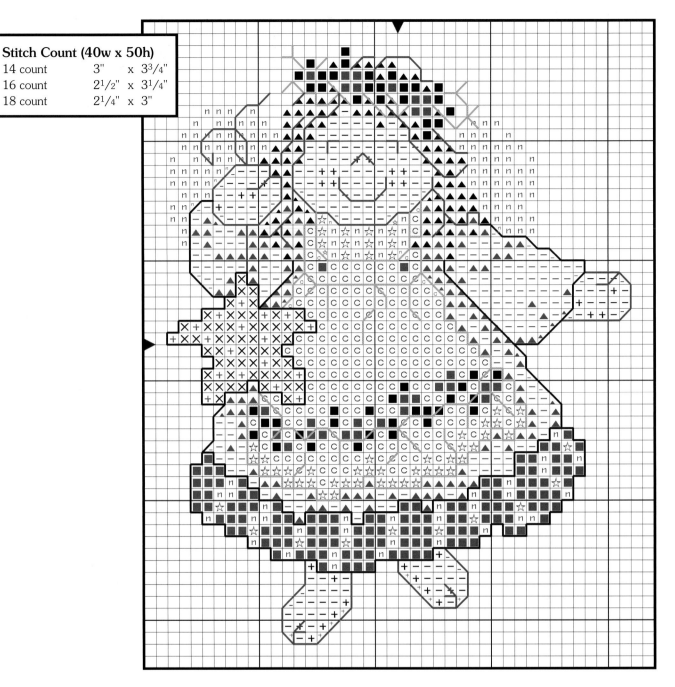

NATIVITY ANGEL

X	DMC	1/4X	B'ST	ANC.	COLOR
☆	blanc	☆		2	white
C	164	C			lt green
n	225	n		1026	pink
■	321		╱	9046	red
▲	436	▲		1045	golden brown
▲	676	▲		891	gold
−	677	╱		886	lt gold
✕	726			295	dk yellow
+	727			293	yellow
+	754	+		1012	peach
	801		╱	359	brown
−	948	╱		1011	lt peach
■	987		╱	244	dk green

Nativity Angel was stitched on a 6" x 6³/4" piece of 14 count White Aida (design size 3" x 3³/4"). Three strands of floss were used for Cross Stitch and one strand for Backstitch.

Shown on page 27.

ANGEL #1

X	DMC	¼X	B'ST	ANC.	COLOR
☆	blanc		/	2	white
▲	321	◢	/	9046	red
■	352			9	peach
+	353	◢		6	lt peach
L	437	◢		362	beige
☒	726			295	yellow
	898		/	360	brown

Angel #1 was stitched on a 5³/₄" x 6¹/₂" piece of 14 count White Aida (design size 2³/₄" x 3¹/₂"). Three strands of floss were used for Cross Stitch and one strand for Backstitch.

Shown on page 27.

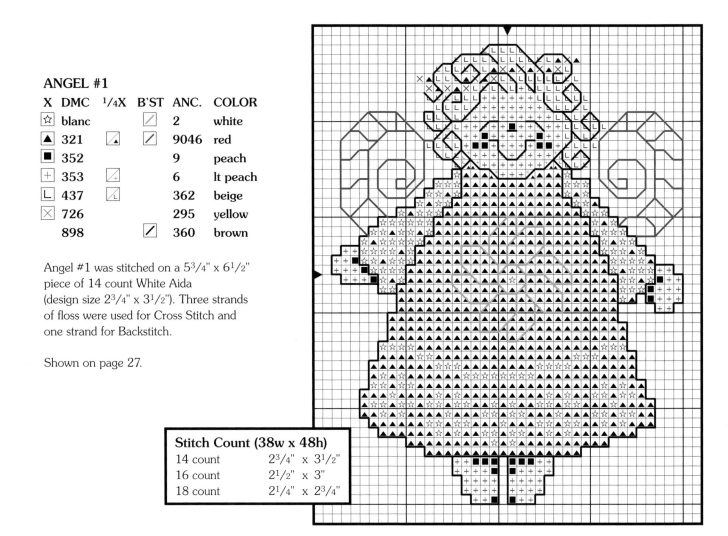

Stitch Count (38w x 48h)
14 count	2³/₄"	x 3¹/₂"
16 count	2¹/₂"	x 3"
18 count	2¹/₄"	x 2³/₄"

Stitch Count (50w x 34h)
14 count	3³/₄"	x 2¹/₂"
16 count	3¹/₄"	x 2¹/₄"
18 count	3"	x 2"

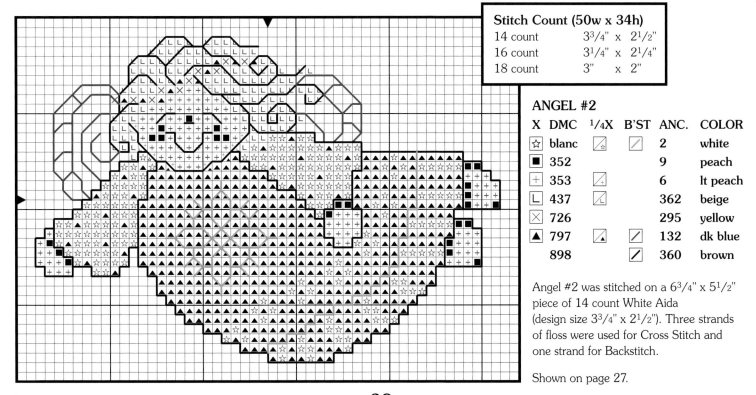

ANGEL #2

X	DMC	¼X	B'ST	ANC.	COLOR
☆	blanc	◢	/	2	white
■	352			9	peach
+	353	◢		6	lt peach
L	437	◢		362	beige
☒	726	◢		295	yellow
▲	797	◢	/	132	dk blue
	898		/	360	brown

Angel #2 was stitched on a 6³/₄" x 5¹/₂" piece of 14 count White Aida (design size 3³/₄" x 2¹/₂"). Three strands of floss were used for Cross Stitch and one strand for Backstitch.

Shown on page 27.

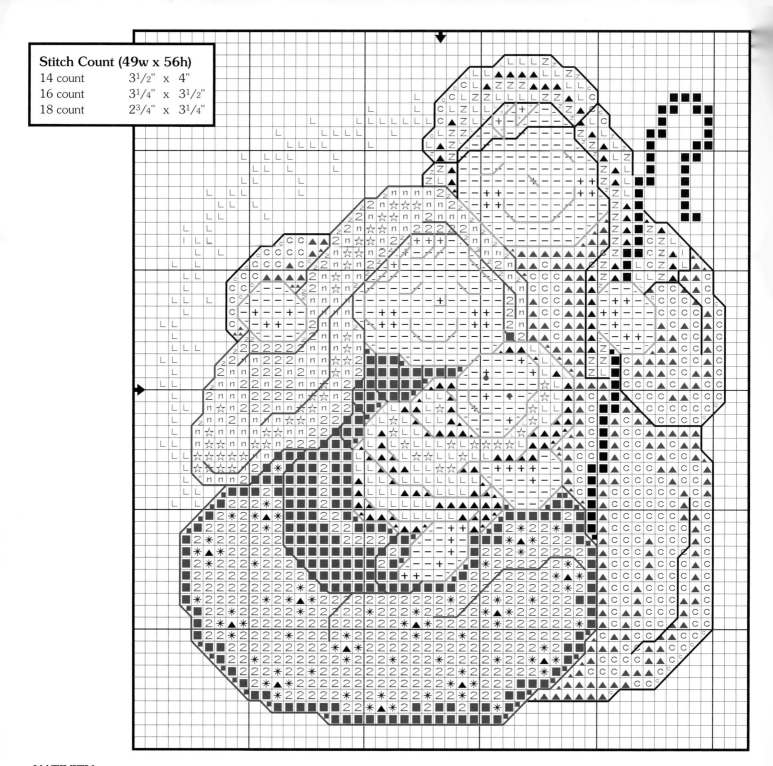

NATIVITY

X	DMC	1/4X	B'ST	ANC.	COLOR		X	DMC	1/4X	B'ST	ANC.	COLOR
☆	blanc			2	white		2	809	⁄		130	lt blue
Z	321	⁄		9046	red					⁄	895	1044	vy dk green
+	435	⁄		1046	dk golden brown		■	898	⁄		360	dk brown
▲	676	⁄		891	gold		–	948	⁄		1011	lt peach
L	677	⁄		886	lt gold		▲	987	⁄		244	dk green
+	754			1012	peach		C	989	⁄		242	green
	796		⁄	133	dk blue		✳	3837			100	purple
■	798	⁄		131	blue		●	898			360	dk brown Fr. Knot
n	800	⁄		144	vy lt blue							

Stitch Count (49w x 56h)

14 count	3 1/2"	x	4"
16 count	3 1/4"	x	3 1/2"
18 count	2 3/4"	x	3 1/4"

Nativity was stitched on a 6 1/2" x 7" piece of 14 count White Aida (design size 3 1/2" x 4"). Three strands of floss were used for Cross Stitch and one strand for Backstitch and French Knots.

Shown on page 27.

40

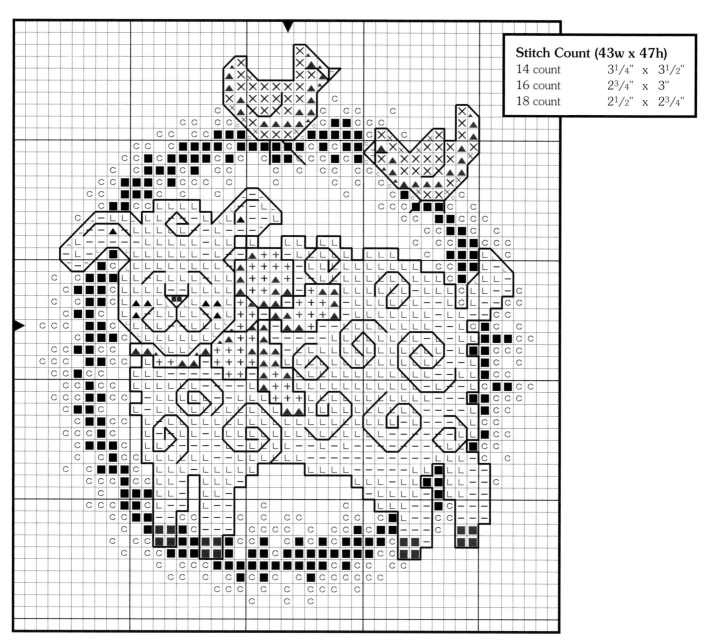

NATIVITY SHEEP

X	DMC	1/4X	B'ST	ANC.	COLOR
▲	321	⊿		9046	red
+	351			10	dk apricot
+	352			9	apricot
✕	498	⊠		1005	red
▲	754			1012	peach
−	842	⊿		1080	beige
■	898	⊿	╱	360	dk brown
■	987			244	dk green
C	989	⊿		242	green
L	3866	⊿		926	off white

Nativity Sheep was stitched on a 6$\frac{1}{4}$" x 6$\frac{1}{2}$" piece of 14 count White Aida (design size 3$\frac{1}{4}$" x 3$\frac{1}{2}$"). Three strands of floss were used for Cross Stitch and one strand for Backstitch.

Shown on page 23.

Stitch Count (43w x 47h)

14 count	3$\frac{1}{4}$"	x	3$\frac{1}{2}$"
16 count	2$\frac{3}{4}$"	x	3"
18 count	2$\frac{1}{2}$"	x	2$\frac{3}{4}$"

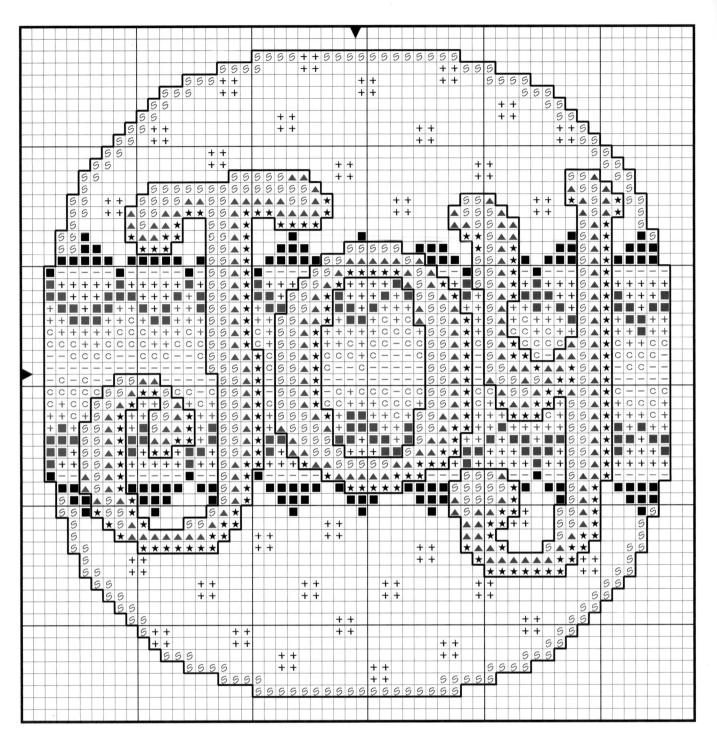

JOY

X	DMC	B'ST	ANC.	COLOR
■	700	╱	228	green
+	703		238	lime green
▲	726		295	dk yellow
৬	727		293	yellow
▣	796		133	dk blue
+	798		131	blue
−	800		144	vy lt blue
C	809		130	lt blue
★	3820		306	dk gold

Joy was stitched on a 7" x 7" piece of
14 count White Aida (design size 4" x 4").
Three strands of floss were used for
Cross Stitch and one strand for Backstitch.

Stitch Count (54w x 54h)			
14 count	4"	x	4"
16 count	3^1/$_2$"	x	3^1/$_2$"
18 count	3"	x	3"

Shown on page 27.

POLAR BEAR

X	DMC	1/4X	B'ST	ANC.	COLOR
■	311	◢		148	blue
■	321			9046	red
	415		╱	398	grey
+	726	◢	╱	295	yellow
+	989			242	green

Polar Bear was stitched on a 7" x 7" piece of 14 count White Aida (design size 4" x 4"). Three strands of floss were used for Cross Stitch and one strand for Backstitch.

Stitch Count (56w x 56h)		
14 count	4"	x 4"
16 count	3 1/2"	x 3 1/2"
18 count	3 1/4"	x 3 1/4"

Shown on page 27.

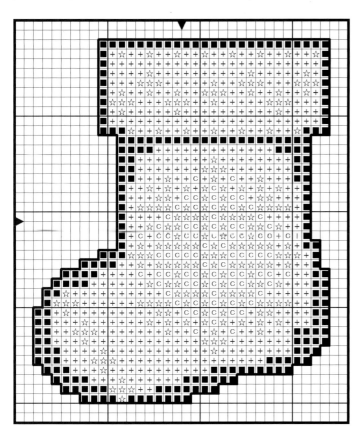

Blue Snowflake Stocking

Green Snowflake Stocking

Stitch Count (32w x 38h)		
14 count	2 1/2"	x	2 3/4"
16 count	2"	x	2 1/2"
18 count	2"	x	2 1/4"

Each Snowflake Stocking was stitched on a 6" x 6 1/2" piece of 11 count White Aida (design size 3" x 3 1/2"). Four strands of floss were used for Cross Stitch and one strand for Backstitch.

SNOWFLAKE STOCKINGS

X	DMC	B'ST	ANC.	COLOR
☆	blanc		2	white
Z	321		9046	red
−	351		10	dk peach
▲	700	╱	228	lt green
C	702		226	lime green
−	704		256	lt lime green
■	796	╱	133	dk blue
+	798		131	blue
C	809		130	lt blue
▲	816	╱	1005	maroon

Shown on page 23.

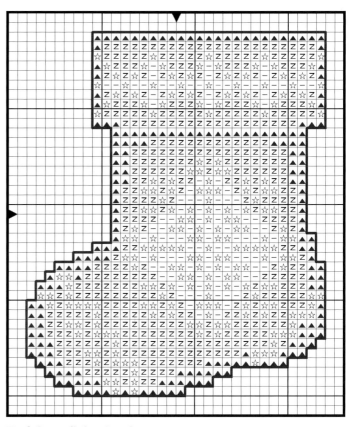

Red Snowflake Stocking

STOCKING #2

X	DMC	B'ST	ANC.	COLOR
■	321		9046	red
C	351		10	dk peach
+	352		9	peach
+	353		6	lt peach
−	677		886	lt gold
2	704		256	lt lime green
L	726		295	yellow
▲	816	/	1005	maroon
■	895		1044	dk avocado green
▲	987		244	avocado green

Stocking #2 was stitched on a 6" x 6¹/₂" piece of
11 count White Aida (design size 3" x 3¹/₂").
Four strands of floss were used for Cross Stitch
and one strand for Backstitch.

Shown on page 23.

Stitch Count (32w x 38h)		
14 count	2¹/₂"	x 2³/₄"
16 count	2"	x 2¹/₂"
18 count	2"	x 2¹/₄"

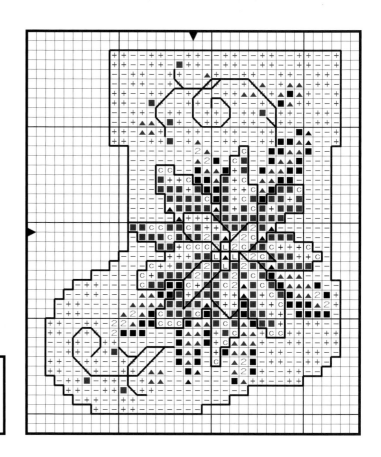

STOCKING #3

X	DMC	¹/₄X	B'ST	ANC.	COLOR
■	321	◢		9046	red
C	351			10	dk peach
+	352			9	peach
−	712	◢		926	cream
L	726			295	yellow
+	739	◢		387	beige
▲	816	◢	/	1005	maroon
■	986	◢		246	dk avocado green
▲	988	◢		243	lt avocado green

Stocking #3 was stitched on a 6" x 6¹/₂" piece
of 11 count White Aida (design size 3" x 3¹/₂").
Four strands of floss were used for Cross Stitch
and one strand for Backstitch.

Shown on page 23.

Stitch Count (32w x 38h)		
14 count	2¹/₂"	x 2³/₄"
16 count	2"	x 2¹/₂"
18 count	2"	x 2¹/₄"

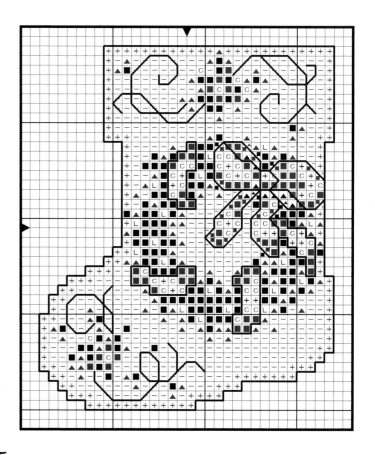

STOCKING #4

X	DMC	1/4X	B'ST	ANC.	COLOR
■	321	◢	╱	9046	red
★	677	◢		886	lt gold
L	726			295	yellow
−	746	◢		275	lt yellow
	816		╱	1005	maroon
■	895	◢		1044	vy dk avocado green
✳	947			330	orange
▲	987	◢		244	avocado green
+	989			242	lt avocado green

Stocking #4 was stitched on a 6" x 6 1/2" piece
of 11 count White Aida (design size 3" x 3 1/2").
Four strands of floss were used for Cross Stitch
and one strand for Backstitch.

Shown on page 23.

Stitch Count (32w x 38h)		
14 count	2 1/2"	x 2 3/4"
16 count	2"	x 2 1/2"
18 count	2"	x 2 1/4"

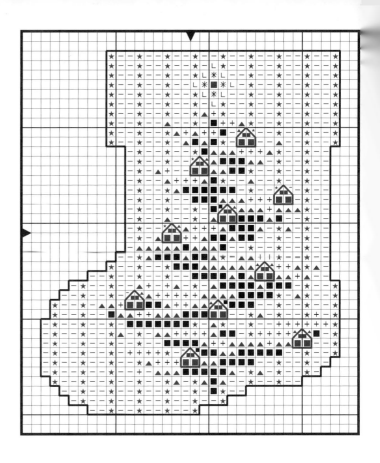

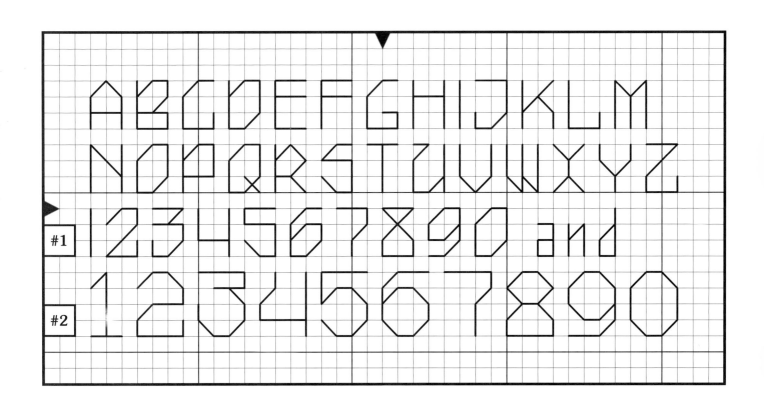

General Instructions

HOW TO READ CHARTS

Each chart is made up of a key and a gridded design on which each square represents a stitch. The symbols in the key tell which floss color to use for each stitch in the chart. The following headings and symbols are given:

    X — Cross Stitch
    DMC — DMC color number
    1/4 X — Quarter Stitch
    B'ST — Backstitch
    ANC. — Anchor color number
    COLOR — The name given to the floss color in this chart

A square filled with a symbol should be worked as a **Cross Stitch**.

A reduced symbol should be worked as a **Quarter Stitch**.

A straight line should be worked as a **Backstitch**.

A large dot listed near the end of the key should be worked as a **French Knot**.

HOW TO STITCH

Always work **Cross Stitches** and **Quarter Stitches** first and then add the **Backstitch** and **French Knots**. When stitching, bring the threaded needle up at 1 and all odd numbers and down at 2 and all even numbers.

Cross Stitch (X): For horizontal rows, work stitches in two journeys **(Fig. 1)**. For vertical rows, complete each stitch as shown **(Fig. 2)**.

Fig. 1

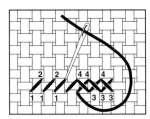

Fig. 2

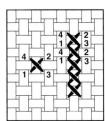

Quarter Stitch (1/4X): Come up at 1, and then split fabric thread to go down at 2 **(Fig. 3)**.

Fig. 3

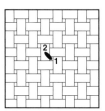

Backstitch (B'ST): For outlines and details, Backstitch should be worked after the design has been completed **(Fig. 4)**.

Fig. 4

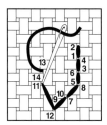

French Knot: Bring the needle up at 1. Wrap the floss once around the needle. Insert the needle at 2, tighten the knot, and pull the needle through the fabric, holding the floss until it must be released **(Fig. 5)**. For a larger knot, use more floss strands and wrap only once.

Fig. 5

47

STITCHING TIPS

Preparing Fabric

Being sure to allow plenty of margin, cut fabric to the desired size and overcast raw edges. It is better to waste a little fabric than to come up short after hours of stitching!

Working with Floss

To ensure smoother stitches, separate strands and realign them before threading the needle. Keep stitching tension consistent. Begin and end floss by running under several stitches on the back; never tie knots.

Dye Lot Variation

It is important to buy all of the floss you need to complete your project from the same dye lot. Although variations in color may be slight when flosses from two different dye lots are held together, the variation is usually apparent on a stitched piece.

Where to Start

The horizontal and vertical centers of each charted design are shown by arrows. You may start at any point on the charted design, but be sure the design will be centered on the fabric. Locate the center of the fabric by folding it in half, top to bottom and again left to right. On the charted design, count the number of squares (stitches) from the center of the chart to where you wish to start. Then from the fabric's center, find your starting point by counting out the same number of fabric threads (stitches).

Fabric provided courtesy of Charles Craft, Inc.
Embroidery floss provided courtesy of The DMC Corporation.

Production Team: Writer – Joyce Scott Harris; Senior Graphic Artist – Chaska Richardson Lucas; Graphic Artist – Karen Allbright; Photo Stylist – Cassie Francioni.

Instructions tested by Muriel Hicks.

Production Services provided by Emerald Ideas.